D0831081

500 741 626

# CAVALIERS AND ROUNDHEADS

WANDSWORTH LIBRARY SERVICE

# CAVALIERS AND ROUNDHEADS

## SIMON ADAMS

## W
## FRANKLIN WATTS
### LONDON•SYDNEY

Illustrations   David Frankland

Designer   Billin Design Solutions
Editor   Penny Clarke
Art Director   Jonathan Hair
Editor-in-Chief   John C. Miles

500741626   C942062 ADAM

© 2002 Franklin Watts

First published in 2002
by Franklin Watts
96 Leonard Street
London
EC2A 4XD

Franklin Watts Australia
56 O'Riordan Street
Alexandria
NSW 2015

ISBN 0 7496 4434 6

Dewey classification: 941.06

A CIP catalogue record
for this book is available
from the British Library.

Printed in Hong Kong/China

# CONTENTS

# Stuart Britain

In 1603 Elizabeth I, queen of England, Wales and Ireland died. Her successor was the Stuart king James VI of Scotland, who now also became James I of England, Wales and Ireland. For the first time, the four nations of the British Isles were ruled by the same person. But what sort of country did he rule?

**"I will govern according to the common weal [good], but not according to the common will."**

James I, December 1621

Parliament controlled its doctrines and forms of worship.

The principality of Wales was governed by England and sent representatives to parliament in London, but it remained quite distinct from England in many ways, with most people speaking the Welsh language.

The fourth part of the country, the kingdom of Ireland, was quite different. It had its own government and parliament, which met in Dublin, and its own legal system. Members of the government and senior officials were Protestant, but most native Irish people were Roman Catholic and owed religious allegiance to the pope in Rome. In Ulster, in Northern Ireland, many people were presbyterian settlers from Scotland. Many more Scots settlers were to arrive in Ulster by the end of the 1630s.

Parliament House

## A UNITED KINGDOM?

When James became king in 1603, the crown was the only thing that united the four nations. Everything else remained separate.

Scotland had its own government, parliament and legal system. It also had its own Protestant church, the presbyterian Kirk, in which the presbyters (priests or ministers) and bishops were elected by church members.

These elections took place in presbyteries and synods (councils). The General Assembly of members of the church agreed its doctrines and forms of worship.

England, too, had its own government and parliament, which met in Westminster, London, and its own legal system. Its church was run by bishops appointed by the king, who was the head of the church.

## WHO GOVERNED THE COUNTRY?

James I believed that he was divinely appointed to rule, and did not accept that parliament had a role in government. In England, however, parliament had become strong and confident under Queen Elizabeth I (reigned 1558-1603). Only parliament could raise taxes and pass laws. It governed the Anglican church and expected to be consulted about foreign policy.

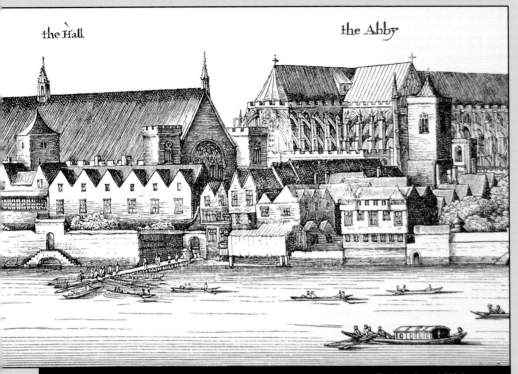

the Hall        the Abby

**The parliament that met at Westminster made laws only for England and Wales.**

At first James was well advised by the Earl of Salisbury, who had been chief minister to Elizabeth I, but his relations with the English parliament were never good. After Salisbury's death in 1612, James increasingly ignored parliament, which met briefly only twice during the rest of his reign. On his death in 1625, James handed over a troubled inheritance to his son, Charles I.

## IS THAT A FACT?

**THE DIVINE RIGHT OF KINGS**
The theory of the divine right of kings began in medieval Europe. People believed that kings were chosen by God to rule the kingdom, and that they were answerable only to God, not the people or parliament, for their actions. It was therefore sinful for the people to resist the king.

Both James I and his son, Charles I, believed in their divine right to rule: James I said in 1610 that "kings are not only God's lieutenants upon earth, and sit upon God's throne, but even by God himself they are called gods."

## FACT FILE

**THE PARTIAL UNIFICATION OF BRITAIN**

**1494** Irish parliament passes Poynings's Law, requiring parliament to seek the English king's permission to meet and to pass legislation

**1536, 1543** Wales is united with England and sends MPs to the House of Commons

**1541** Henry VIII of England declares himself king (rather than Lord) of Ireland

**1603** Elizabeth I of England dies; her heir is James of Scotland. The three thrones are now united, although parliaments, laws and churches are separate

**1604-11** First English parliament of the new reign clashes repeatedly with James

**1611-25** James tries to rule England without parliament, which he summons only twice

**1621** English parliament meets briefly and clashes with the king again; it agrees a Protestation that its privileges are "the ancient and undoubted birthright...of the subjects of England." James tears the Protestation out of the House of Commons record book

**1625** James dies and is succeeded by his son, Charles

# The rule of Charles I

When Charles I died in 1649, one woman wrote that "men wondered that so good a man should be so bad a king." But how bad was he?

## BATTLES WITH PARLIAMENT

In private Charles had great personal charm and modesty and was devoted to his family. In public, however, he was shy and had no sense of humour. Above all, he was stubborn, for he believed that he alone had the right to rule and would not compromise his beliefs in any way.

For the first three years of his reign, Charles relied on the Duke of Buckingham for advice. However, Buckingham's disastrous foreign policy — including failed wars against both Spain and France — led to conflict with the English parliament, which only granted Charles tonnage and poundage money — customs revenues on wine and on the value of all imports and exports — for one year, rather than for life as was traditional.

In 1626 MPs tried to impeach Buckingham, but Charles saved him by dismissing parliament. Charles constantly tried to increase his power at the expense of parliament, but was forced in 1628 to agree to the Petition of Right, a declaration by parliament of the "rights and liberties of the subject" against royal power. Further conflicts continued after Buckingham's assassination in 1628.

> ## "The devil go with the king and all the proud pack of them. What care I?"
>
> **Yorkshire village blacksmith, 1633**

## THE ELEVEN YEARS' TYRANNY

By 1629 Charles had had enough of the English parliament and failed to call another for 11 years. However, only parliament had the right to raise taxes, so Charles had to look elsewhere for money. He revived many of the crown's money-gathering rights which had lapsed, such as fining landowners who had taken over royal forests or common land without consent and all men worth £40 a year or more who had not become knights at Charles's coronation in 1626.

Despite the lack of parliamentary approval, Charles continued to collect tonnage and poundage. Most controversially, he collected "ship money" for the defence of coastal counties from inland counties as well. In 1637 John Hampden, an opponent of the king, refused to pay ship money, but the judges found narrowly in favour of the king. To enforce his personal rule, Charles used the courts of Star Chamber and High Commission — civil and church courts — to suppress opposition.

The main opposition faced by Charles was over his religious policies. Charles favoured a strongly episcopal form of church government. He appointed William Laud Archbishop of Canterbury to reform church practice and ritual. In 1637 he extended these policies to Scotland, causing unrest. By 1640, Charles was faced with rebellion in Scotland and Ireland, and reluctantly recalled parliament.

A 17th-century engraving of Charles. His "personal rule" alienated many.

# HENRIETTA MARIA

Henrietta Maria (1609-1669) was the youngest daughter of Henry IV of France. She married Charles in 1625, but the couple did not fall in love until 1628. From then on, she worked devotedly for Charles, raising money for his military campaigns and attempting to persuade him to be more flexible in his negotiations with parliament. However, she was always distrusted in England because she was a Roman Catholic and tried to convert her six children to Catholicism.

## FACT FILE

EVENTS OF THE REIGN
1625-1640

1625 Charles becomes king of England and Wales, Ireland and Scotland

1625 War begins against Spain

1626 English parliament tries to impeach Charles's main adviser, the Duke of Buckingham

1627 Disastrous war against France

1628 Charles reluctantly agrees to the Petition of Right

1628 Buckingham is assassinated

1629 Charles dissolves the English parliament and rules without it for 11 years

1629 Charles makes peace with France and, in 1630, Spain

1633 William Laud appointed Archbishop of Canterbury

1634 Ship money levied on coastal counties and then, in 1635, on inland counties as well

1637 John Hampden fails in his protest against ship money

1637 Scots object to Charles's policies

1640 Charles recalls the English parliament

# Scotland and Ireland rebel

As Charles continued to rule without parliament in England and Wales, first the Scots and then the Irish rebelled against his religious policies. These two rebellions eventually led to war throughout Britain.

## "That glorious marriage day of the kingdom with God."

Sir Archibald Johnstone signing the Covenant, 1638

## SCOTLAND

Throughout his long reign as king of Scotland (1567–1625), James VI had tried to bring the Kirk under the control of the crown. Charles I intensified his father's policies and was determined that the Kirk should move from its part-presbyterian, part-episcopal structure to an entirely episcopal church similar to the Church of England.

He instructed Archbishop William Laud to prepare a modified version of the English prayer book for use in Scotland.

When the prayer book was first used on Sunday 23 July 1637, riots broke out in St Giles Cathedral, Edinburgh, and in many other churches throughout Scotland.

Opponents of the new prayer book feared that Charles wanted to make their church episcopal, or even Roman Catholic, and drew up the Supplication and Complaint. When Charles ordered the arrest of its authors, his opponents drew up the National Covenant in favour of a presbyterian church.

Both Charles and the Covenanters, as supporters of the Covenant were known, prepared for war.

The Covenanters struck first, seizing major towns across Scotland in March 1639. They defeated both an anti-Covenanter force and a royalist invasion from England. Charles backed down and agreed peace terms.

## IRELAND

Since 1633 Ireland had been governed by Sir Thomas Wentworth. He strengthened the king's control over the island using similar tactics to those used by Charles in England.

## STRAFFORD

Thomas Wentworth (1593-1641) was a parliamentary opponent of Charles until the king made him a baronet in 1628 (and 1st Earl of Strafford in 1640) and appointed him president of the Council of the North. In 1633 he became Lord Deputy of Ireland, where he worked to strengthen Charles's rule. He tried to bring the Church of Ireland into line with the policies of William Laud in England, and was sympathetic to Roman Catholics. In 1639 he returned to London to help Charles in his conflicts with Scotland, but he had made many powerful enemies, and was tried and executed by the English parliament for waging war against Scotland in 1641.

Thousands thronged Tower Hill in London to watch Strafford's execution in 1641.

The independent Irish church was brought more into line with the English church and Irish parliamentary opposition was crushed.

When the Covenanter rebellion broke out in Scotland, Wentworth supported an Irish invasion of Scotland on Charles's behalf. As relations between Charles and the Covenanters broke down again in 1640, he got the Irish parliament to agree to finance Charles.

Wentworth also assembled a large army to invade Scotland. However, a Covenanter army seized the initiative and, before the king could invade, crossed the English border and defeated the royalist army at Newburn, in Northumberland. Charles now gave up attempts to control the Kirk and sued for peace.

By 1641 Charles had also lost control over Ireland and Wentworth, now Earl of Strafford, was in trouble.

In May, Wentworth was arrested, tried and executed by the English parliament for waging war against Scotland.

Irish Catholics in Ulster seized this opportunity to rise in rebellion against Protestant colonists who had taken their land. The rebellion quickly spread to other parts of the island.

By early 1642 two parts of the kingdom were in open rebellion against the king.

## FACT FILE

EVENTS OF THE REIGN
1637-1641

July 1637  Riots break out in Scotland

October 1637 Supplication and Complaint drawn up

February 1638  Scots sign National Covenant

November 1638 General Assembly of the Kirk agrees the National Covenant; both sides prepare for war

March 1639 Covenanters seize Scottish cities

May 1639  First Bishops' War leads to Covenanter victory. Treaty of Berwick ends the war in June

March 1640 Irish parliament agrees to finance Charles's renewed war

July 1640 Strafford's army prepares to invade Scotland

August 1640 Second Bishops' War; king's army defeated

October 1640 Treaty of Ripon ends Second Bishops' War

May 1641 Strafford tried and executed

October 1641 Irish Catholics rebel against Protestant settlers

# Heading for war

Charles was forced to summon a new parliament in 1640. Within two years Britain was on the brink of war. Why?

**"I see all the birds are flown."**

Charles I in the House of Commons,
6 January 1642

The ritual of Black Rod knocking to gain entry to the House of Commons at the State Opening of Parliament dates from Charles's attempt to arrest five MPs in 1642.

## THE SHORT PARLIAMENT

In early 1640 Charles once again prepared for war against the Scottish Covenanters. To do this he needed money to pay his armies. Strafford arranged for money from the Irish parliament, but advised the king to summon the English parliament to raise the large amounts of money he would need to mount an effective campaign in Scotland.

The king reluctantly agreed and the new parliament met on 13 April 1640. However, led by John Pym, it refused to grant the king any money before its grievances against Charles were settled. The king refused and the Short Parliament was dissolved on 5 May.

During the summer, however, the Second Bishops' War with the Covenanters ended in a decisive defeat for Charles. Under the Treaty of Ripon, Charles agreed to pay the Scottish army, which was occupying the north of England, £850 a day out of English taxes.

This was to last until the English parliament agreed to the treaty. So Charles had to call parliament again.

## THE LONG PARLIAMENT

The Long Parliament met in November 1640 and quickly set to work asserting its power.

# PYM

John Pym MP (c.1584-1643) was strongly opposed to the authoritarian rule of both James I and Charles I, making such fierce attacks on Buckingham's foreign policy in parliament that he was placed under house arrest by the government for three months in 1622.

Pym was a clever speaker who won support by argument rather than emotion. He was therefore the natural choice to lead the opposition to Charles in the parliaments of 1640, preparing the impeachment of Strafford and Laud and promoting the legislation of 1641 which broke the king's power. Not suprisingly, he was one of the five MPs the king tried to arrest in January 1642.

The courts of Star Chamber and High Commission were abolished, a Triennial Act forced the king to summon parliament at least once every three years, another act prevented the Long Parliament being dissolved without its own consent, ship money was abolished, tonnage and poundage reduced, and other royal powers abolished.

Strafford, as we have seen, was impeached and executed for treason, as was Archbishop Laud, who was beheaded in 1645.

These and many other measures were revolutionary in nature, for they gave parliament immense new powers at the expense of the king, who lost many of his traditional and ancient rights and privileges.

After a short recess, parliament resumed work in October 1641. However, its unity against the king broke down over reform of the English church. Extremists favoured "root and branch" reform to make the church presbyterian; moderates wanted only limited reform.

Pym also demanded parliamentary control over the king's ministers and over the armed forces, which were needed to suppress the Irish rebellion. When Charles refused, Pym published the Grand Remonstrance against Charles. MPs passed it by a majority of only 11 votes.

Charles rejected it and on 4 January 1642, he arrived at the House of Commons with 400 soldiers to arrest the five most troublesome MPs, including Pym. They, however, had fled to the safety of the City of London. Six days later, the king and his family left London as war seemed likely.

## FACT FILE

EVENTS OF THE REIGN 1640-1642

March 1640 Irish parliament agrees to finance Charles's renewed war against the Covenanters

April-May 1640 Short Parliament refuses to grant Charles money until its grievances are settled

November 1640 Charles forced to summon the Long Parliament

Feb 1641 Triennial Act forces Charles to summon parliament once every three years

May 1641 Strafford is tried and executed by parliament

May 1641 Act ensures parliament cannot be dissolved without its own consent

July 1641 Courts of Star Chamber and High Commission abolished

August 1641 Ship money abolished

October 1641 Irish Catholics rebel against English rule

November 1641 Parliament agrees the Grand Remonstrance, but Charles rejects it

January 1642 Charles tries to arrest 5 MPs but fails; he leaves London as both sides prepare for war

# Four nations at war

After Charles's failure to seize his leading opponents in the House of Commons in January 1642, both sides prepared for war.

> **"All the counties of England were no longer idle spectators, but several stages whereon the tragedy of the civil war was acted."**
>
> **Lucy Hutchinson, 1643**

## WAR BEGINS

Supporters of the king became known as royalists, or cavaliers, a word first used in 1641. A *cavaliere* is an Italian knightly horseman, and the term was originally abusive, as it implied that the royalists were both military fanatics and Roman Catholics. Royalists soon adopted the term as they liked its implications of dashing glamour and gallantry. Roundheads, the abusive term by which the Puritans or supporters of parliament became known, referred to their short hair.

By early 1642 both sides tried to increase their strength by controlling the local militia — groups of part-time soldiers who dealt with emergencies — and seizing arms from army camps and naval bases.

The official declaration of war was made by Charles on 22 August 1642 at Nottingham Castle. He raised a royalist army from Wales and northern England, while the parliamentarians raised an army — led by the Earl of Essex — from the south and east of England.

The first major battle, at Edgehill in Warwickshire, was on 23 October, and was inconclusive. Both sides then tried to capture territory and supplies; further battles took place across England.

Crucially, however, Charles failed to capture London and was turned back at Turnham Green, southwest of London, on 13 November.

## THE WAR WIDENS

Both sides looked for allies. In June 1642 the different groups of Irish rebels had joined forces in the Confederation of Kilkenny and offered peace terms to the king. These were agreed in September 1643 (the Cessation), allowing Charles's army in Ireland to return to England.

## THE TWO SIDES

Charles was not an effective war leader, as he was unable to think quickly or act decisively and did not inspire trust. He did, however, have the support of most landowners, who were able to raise private armies on his behalf. But these commanders were unable to work well together and Charles failed to provide any co-ordination.

The parliamentarians had to raise their own army, but did have control over most of the militia. With the creation of the New Model Army in 1645, they developed a fighting force led by able commanders that was more than a match for the royalist forces.

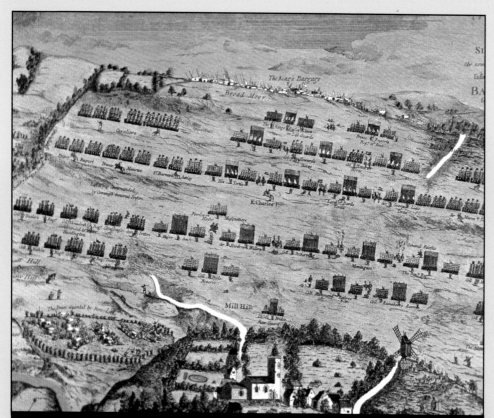

This engraving shows the way in which the royalist army (top) and the New Model Army (bottom) arranged their forces at the decisive battle of Naseby in 1645.

## FACT FILE

EVENTS OF THE WAR
1642-1645

August 1642  Civil war breaks out as king raises his standard

October 1642  First major battle at Edgehill is inconclusive

November 1642 Charles fails to capture London

September 1643  The Cessation ends fighting in Ireland

September 1643 Parliament and Scots ally in Solemn League and Covenant

September 1643 Parliamentarians win battle of Newbury

June 1644  Catholic Irish troops land in Scotland

July 1644  Scots and parliamentarians win battle of Marston Moor

September 1644 Covenanter army defeated in Scotland

December 1644 Self-Denying Ordinance states that membership of parliament is incompatible with military command, thus separating the English parliament from the army

February 1645  New Model Army created

June 1645  New Model Army wins decisive battle of Naseby

At the same time, the English parliament agreed an alliance with the Scottish Covenanters. Both sides now had far larger armies at their disposal.

In January 1644 a Scottish army invaded England, while the royalists won a number of victories. The two sides met on 2 July at Marston Moor, Yorkshire, where the royalists — led by Prince Rupert, Charles's nephew — suffered a major defeat.

However, the royalists had more luck in Scotland, when an Irish army invaded the country in June 1644 and fought with a royalist army against the Covenanters.

The year 1645 proved to be decisive. Parliament had suffered because of its lack of a single, effective army, and was divided in its policies and aims. It therefore decided to merge all existing armies into a "New Model Army".

It was decided that the leaders of this new army would be outside parliament, but under its control. Sir Thomas Fairfax was in command, with Oliver Cromwell as second-in-command.

Four months later, on 14 June, the New Model Army defeated the royalist forces at Naseby. Further defeats at Chester and Bristol, and the refusal of the Welsh to supply any more troops to the king, spelt the end of the royalist cause.

# The war continues

**After the battle of Naseby, the king's military strength decreased. But it was another six years before peace finally returned to Britain.**

## ATTEMPTS AT PEACE

Although Naseby was a major defeat for the king, he had not yet lost the war. In Scotland, the Covenanters were losing ground to the royalist army of the Marquis of Montrose, while in Ireland the Cessation of September 1643 had ended the rebellion, allowing Charles to start secret negotiations with the Confederation.

However, continuing parliamentary victories in 1645 and early 1646, and the destruction of Montrose's army by the Covenanters in September 1645, meant that Charles was losing support fast. By the end of 1645, only Ireland, parts of Wales and western England remained royalist.

Charles therefore took a gamble. The Covenanters were annoyed with the English parliament for failing to fulfil the Solemn League and Covenant of 1643, which they thought meant the establishment of a presbyterian church in England. Charles hoped to exploit this. In disguise, he rode to the Scottish camp at Newark, Nottinghamshire, where he surrendered on 5 May.

He hoped to negotiate with the Scots alone, but they insisted that the English parliament should also be involved. In July the English parliament presented the king with the Newcastle Propositions, which would have introduced the presbyterian church into England and reduced the king's role. Charles rejected the terms.

In January 1647 the Scottish army withdrew and handed the king over to parliament. Charles continued in his attempts to divide his enemies, who were themselves already divided. The Scots were split between Covenanters and royalists; the army was increasingly split between its leaders, the Grandees, and its radical rank and file, and the English parliament was split between presbyterians and Independents.

In March 1647 the English parliament suggested that, now the war against the king appeared to be over, the New Model Army disband and its soldiers join a new army to fight the Irish.

## FAIRFAX

Thomas Fairfax (1612-71) was a brilliant military commander. Although knighted by King Charles in 1641, he joined the parliamentary side in 1642 and led his army to victory at Marston Moor in 1644. As Lord General of the New Model Army in 1645, he led the army to victory again at Naseby.

In the late 1640s, he became unhappy at the militancy of the army and played no part in Charles's trial. He sat in parliament for most of the 1650s and was one of those who recalled Charles II to the throne in 1660.

As a result, many regiments grew restless. In June 1647 a cavalry unit led by Cornet George Joyce seized the king and took him to Newmarket.

Led by Cromwell, the army now offered the king its own peace terms: the Heads of the Proposals, which abolished the Church of England but did not impose a replacement.

They also gave the king considerable power. Charles rejected the terms and, in November, escaped from army control and fled to Carisbrooke Castle on the Isle of Wight. There he negotiated the Engagement with the Scots, under which he agreed to accept a presbyterian church for three years while the Scots sent an army to restore him to power.

The English parliament promptly passed the Vote of No Addresses (no communication) with the king, making renewed civil war inevitable.

## THE SECOND CIVIL WAR

In February 1648 a rebellion broke out among soldiers at Pembroke Castle in Wales against the New Model Army's domination of government. By May it became a second civil war as many parts of the country — notably Kent and Essex — rose in rebellion and declared for the king.

Led by General Fairfax, the New Model Army defeated the English rebels at Maidstone, Kent in June and at Colchester, Essex in August. Cromwell's army crushed the Welsh rebellion in July; the invading Scots were defeated in August. The second English civil war was over, but the problem of what to do about the king was now very urgent.

## RUPERT

Prince Rupert of the Rhine (1619-82) was the nephew of Charles I. He was a daring, skilful soldier who, at the outbreak of the civil wars in 1642, was made general of the horse and then commander-in-chief of the royalist armies. He took part in all the major battles of the First English Civil War but was defeated at both Marston Moor in 1644 and at Naseby in 1645.
Charles lost confidence in him when he surrendered control of the royalist port of Bristol to parliament and he was dismissed in 1645. He later took control of the royalist navy.

## FACT FILE

**EVENTS OF THE WAR 1645-1648**

**July 1645** King starts secret negotiations with Confederation

**September 1645** Covenanters defeat Montrose's army

**May 1646** Charles surrenders to Covenanters

**July 1646** Parliament presents Charles with Newcastle Propositions

**January 1647** Scots hand Charles over to parliament

**June 1647** Army troop led by Cornet Joyce seizes king

**August 1647** Army leaders offer Charles the Heads of the Proposals

**November 1647** Charles flees to Carisbrooke Castle

**December 1647** Charles signs Engagement with the Scots

**January 1648** Parliament passes Vote of No Addresses, ending all negotiations

**February-May 1648** Rebellion breaks out in South Wales, Kent and other parts of England

**July 1648** Scottish Engager army invades England

**August 1648** Cromwell defeats Engager and royalist army at Preston

# An upside-down world

During the 1640s, England erupted in revolutionary ferment. It was as if, in the words of Christopher Hill, a modern historian, "the world turned upside down".

> "Trust your great officers . . . no farther than you can throw an ox."
>
> John Lilburne to the army rank and file, August 1647

## A FREE PRESS

The abolition of the Court of High Commission in July 1641 meant that control over the press came to an end. Many new newspapers soon appeared. Royalist papers in Oxford, headquarters of the king, and parliamentary papers in London argued their causes. Radical religious and political groups took advantage of the new freedom to produce pamphlets. As a result, lively debate sprang up across the country.

The main debate was about religion. Royalists supported the existing episcopal government of the church but many parliamentarians wanted to introduce presbyterianism, as in Scotland. Some, however, did not want any form of national church and preferred to let congregations organise themselves free of state control. The Independents, as they were known, shared many beliefs with the Levellers, a radical political movement which grew up in the early 1640s. The Levellers drew their support from working people in London and southern England and from the ranks of the army. Their opponents called them Levellers because they were accused of wanting to end all class distinctions.

## POLITICAL DEBATE

Much political debate took place inside the army. The New Model Army had been set up by a presbyterian-dominated parliament but was led by Independents and contained many Independents and Levellers in its ranks. During 1646, parliament was unable to pay the army and the soldiers grew critical of its leadership. When parliament suggested in March 1647 that, because the king was in parliamentary hands, the New Model Army should disband, soldiers elected agitators, or representatives, to discuss political action. They circulated petitions and campaigned for back pay and other rights, such as compensation for widows and dependants.

Parliament's announcement in May 1647 that the army would disband the next month caused Cornet Joyce to seize the king while the army itself marched to London to force concessions from parliament. Conflict between an Independent army and a presbyterian parliament, supported by Londoners, seemed inevitable. As the army leaders presented their Heads of the Proposals to the king, army radicals drew up their own proposals, while the Levellers proposed democratic government, adult male suffrage, abolition of the House of Lords, and a republic.

After August 1647, the army dominated parliament but it was itself divided between its more cautious senior leaders — Fairfax, Cromwell and Commissary-General Henry Ireton, known as the Grandees — and its radical soldiers. Together with the Levellers, all sides met at Putney to thrash out their differences. The debate was wide-ranging, but it was brought to end without conclusion when Charles escaped from captivity.

The interior of St Mary's Church, Putney, where the Putney Debates were held.

## REVOLUTIONARY EVENTS 1641-1647

**July 1641** Abolition of the Court of High Commission ends press censorship

**1646** Levellers publish A Remonstrance of Many Thousand Citizens, a pamphlet attacking parliament

**March 1647** Parliament proposes to disband the New Model Army, which now becomes increasingly political

**June 1647** Army marches on London

**23 July 1647** Army leaders present their Heads of the Proposals to the king

**August 1647** Army occupies London; parliament expels its main presbyterian members

**September 1647** Army radicals publish their own proposals – The Case of the Army Truly Stated

**October 1647** Levellers publish the radical Agreement of the People

**Oct-Nov 1647** Army officers, agitators, Independents and Levellers meet at St Mary's Church, Putney to debate their ideas

**November 1647** King escapes from captivity

# LILBURNE

### JOHN LILBURNE

John Lilburne (c.1614-57) was a political activist and member of the Levellers. He was imprisoned in 1638-40 for importing banned puritan books and fought for the parliamentary army when war broke out.

He left the army in 1645 and became one of the main leaders of the Levellers, using his great skill as a writer and propagandist to advance their cause. He was frequently imprisoned for his beliefs by the government, and in April 1649 was tried but acquitted of acting against the state.

# Execution of the king

When Charles escaped from army captivity in November 1647, he hoped to regain his throne and his power. In little more than a year, however, he had lost his life.

> **"Charles Stuart, King of England, you are accused on behalf of the Commons of England of divers high crimes and treasons."**
> The formal charge against Charles, 23 January 1649

## THE ARMY IN CONTROL

In late 1647 the army Grandees had crushed Leveller-inspired mutinies in their ranks and reasserted their control over their radical troops.

During the Second Civil War (1648), the army had defeated the invading Scots and subsequently crushed rebellions by the royalists and within their own ranks in England and Wales.

### A KING'S DEFENCE

An extract from Charles I's speech on the scaffold, 30 January 1649.

"Truly I desire (the people's) liberty and freedom as much as anybody: but I must tell you, that their liberty and freedom consists in having government of those laws, by which their life and their goods may be most their own; it is not for having a share in government, that is nothing pertaining to them. A subject and sovereign are clean different things. . ."

By the end of August 1648, the Independent-dominated army controlled the country and wanted no more negotiations with the king. The presbyterian-dominated parliament, however, wanted to squash any radical proposals from the army and hoped that a defeated Charles would accept proposals for peace.

They suspended the Vote of No Addresses and reopened negotiations on the same terms as the Newcastle Propositions of July 1646, which would have introduced a presbyterian church into England. Charles, meanwhile, still hoped that Irish forces would come to his rescue.

Faced with this situation, the Grandees took their own decision.

Many of them remembered the suggestion during the Putney Debates that Charles was a "Man of Blood" and should pay for his crimes with his life. On 20 November 1648 the army demanded that "the capital and grand author of our troubles, the person of the king . . . may be speedily brought to justice for the treason, blood and mischief he is guilty of."

When parliament ignored this demand, the army reoccupied London and one of its members, Colonel Pride, evicted from parliament those presbyterian members who wished to continue discussions with the king.

In effect, the army had mounted a military coup against the elected parliament and now ran the country.

## THE TRIAL

The Rump Parliament, as it was known, moved fast to carry out the army's wishes.

It set up a High Court of Justice to try the king, and redefined high treason as an offence to "levy war against the Parliament and Kingdom of England" — the existing law stated that it was treason to fight against the king, which Charles obviously could not have done! A charge of high treason automatically carried the death penalty.

Parliament claimed the right to try the king on behalf of the people because he had abused the trust of his people.

When the trial started on 21 January 1649, however, Charles refused to recognise the legitimacy of the court and was eloquent in his arguments. Many agreed with him, and in the end only 59 of the 135 commissioners of the High Court who heard the case felt able to sign the death warrant.

This was a show-trial and its conclusion was not in doubt. Charles's execution took place outside the Banqueting Hall in Whitehall, central London.

**THE EXECUTION OF THE KING**

**November 1647** King Charles escapes from army custody

**November 1647** Grandees crush Leveller-inspired mutinies

**May-August 1648** Second Civil War leads to royalist defeat

**September 1648** Parliament reopens talks with the king

**November 1648** Army submits the Remonstrance of the Army to parliament

**2 December 1648** Army reoccupies London

**6 December 1648** Colonel Pride purges parliament of its presbyterian members

**1 January 1649** Rump Parliament introduces new definition of treason

**4 January 1649** House of Commons claims authority to act on behalf of the people without the king or House of Lords

**6 January 1649** Court set up to try the king

**21-27 January 1649** Trial of the king begins; Charles found guilty

**30 January 1649** Charles is executed in London

The execution of King Charles took place on a bitterly cold January day in London.

# The Commonwealth

The execution of the king solved one problem, but it caused many more as the English parliament and the army struggled to set up the new republic.

## "A crowning mercy"
Cromwell on his victory at Worcester,
September 1651

## WHAT NEXT?

Charles I had been king of four nations — England and Wales, Scotland, and Ireland — but only the English parliament had tried and executed him, and in the name of the people of England only. Both the Scots and the Irish were angry at his death and proclaimed Charles I's son king as Charles II.

In London, the Rump Parliament faced four main tasks. These were constructing a republic, dealing with internal enemies, crushing the continuing rebellion in Ireland, and subduing Scotland.

It quickly abolished the monarchy and the House of Lords, set up a Council of State to govern the country, and in May 1649 declared England and Wales a Commonwealth and Free State, or a republic.

The head of the new Council of State was Oliver Cromwell. Under his leadership all traces of the old royal government were swept aside. Internal enemies were also dealt with swiftly: royalist prisoners were brought to trial and some were executed, although most were fined or had their property confiscated. Some Levellers were also imprisoned because they had protested against the army.

Twice, Katherine Chidley, a London Leveller, and Elizabeth Lilburne, wife of John, presented petitions to parliament demanding their release — the second petition had 10,000 signatures — and twice parliament rejected them. Leading Levellers called for the Putney Debates to restart, but when some soldiers mutinied in their favour, the army attacked the Levellers at Burford, Oxfordshire, and executed three.

## RADICAL GROUPS

In 1649 a number of new and extreme groups appeared in England. The True Levellers, better known as the Diggers, believed that God gave the earth to everyone to share and that everyone should therefore work on the land. In March 1649 they established a colony at St George's Hill, outside Weybridge in Surrey, as well as others in southern England. They were peaceful, but they rejected ownership of property, threatening the basis of wealth and power in England. Many of their colonies were broken up by armed gangs hired by landowners.

New religious sects also appeared. The Ranters believed there was no such thing as sin, and since God had created every aspect of human life, it was not a sin to be sexually promiscuous. Both Diggers and Ranters attracted considerable attention, but neither had the impact of the Levellers.

## IRELAND AND SCOTLAND

The main military threat to the new republic came from Ireland. Here the Catholic-dominated Confederation of Kilkenny had allied with Irish royalists, whose ships were using Irish ports to attack ships of the new English republic.

In August 1649 Cromwell landed in Ireland to crush the rebellion. He stormed Drogheda in September, massacring many of its citizens, and did the same at Wexford the following month. This brutality had the desired effect, and by June 1650, most of Ireland — except the far west — was in English hands.

In May 1650 Cromwell returned to England to face the Scots, who had reached an agreement with Charles II. Cromwell's army marched north and in September 1650 defeated the Scottish army at Dunbar.

**Cromwell led the New Model Army to victory over the Scots at Dunbar in September 1650.**

The Scots, however, regrouped and led by Charles II invaded England in July 1651. However, Charles II failed to gain much support, as the English were tired of war, and his army was easily defeated at Worcester. In 1652, as a result of this defeat, Scotland joined the Commonwealth; its parliament and government were abolished and its MPs now sat at Westminster. Ireland was forcibly united with England, its parliament abolished, and Catholic landowners punished for their rebellion. Ireland now became a mere colony of England.

# FACT FILE

**THE COMMONWEALTH 1649-1653**

**February 1649** Charles II proclaimed king in Scotland and Ireland

**February 1649** Council of State set up to govern the country

**March 1649** Monarchy and House of Lords abolished

**April-May 1649** Women petition for release of Leveller prisoners

**May 1649** Leveller mutiny put down at Burford, Oxfordshire

**May 1649** England and Wales declared a Commonwealth

**Sept-Oct 1649** Cromwell takes Drogheda and Wexford

**June 1650** Final defeat of Irish armies

**September 1650** Scots defeated by Cromwell at Dunbar

**July 1651** Charles II invades England

**Sept-Oct 1651** Charles II defeated at Worcester; escapes next month to France

**April 1652** Scotland joins Commonwealth

**August 1652** Act of Settlement unites Ireland with England and evicts Catholic landowners

# The Protectorate

Although Cromwell now dominated Britain, he was unable to devise a system of government which had popular consent yet which would not challenge his own power.

> "You have sat too long here for any good you have been doing. Depart, I say, and let us have done with you. In the name of God, go!"
>
> Cromwell dismissing the Rump Parliament, 20 April 1653

## THE PROTECTORATE

The Long Parliament had sat, without new elections, since 1640 — throughout the war. Most members had been purged in 1648 to create the "Rump" Parliament, which was was deeply unpopular.

The Rump refused to carry out reforms or resign and be replaced. It had also not raised enough taxes to pay the army's wages. On 20 April 1653 Cromwell and a group of soldiers entered the House of Commons and expelled its members.

The new parliament became known as the Little, or Barebones Parliament, after "Praise-God" Barbon, or Barebones, one of its members.
This parliament first met in July 1653. Its members were drawn from all four nations, making it the first true parliament of the British Isles. It too failed to win support and was dissolved in December.

In its place a new constitution established the Protectorate, with Cromwell styled as "Lord Protector".

In addition there was a Council of State and a parliament drawn from all four nations of Britain.

This new parliament, however, soon tried to gain control over the Council of State, and so Cromwell dissolved it in 1655 and, after an unsuccessful royalist revolt, appointed 11 major-generals to run the country.

This attempt at direct military rule was deeply unpopular and Cromwell was forced once again to summon a new parliament. The second Protectorate Parliament was more successful, abolishing the major-generals and introducing a new constitution.
This was called the Humble Petition and Advice.

Some MPs wanted to make Cromwell king, but he refused.

However, when parliament began attacking Cromwell's supporters in the Other House (the replacement for the House of Lords), Cromwell lost patience and dissolved this parliament too.

Before he had time to summon a new parliament, Cromwell died at Whitehall in September 1658 after a brief illness.

## SUCCESS AND FAILURE

Although the Protectorate failed to establish a stable government, it did have some successes. At home, the church became more tolerant of a range of beliefs, while Jews were readmitted to Britain for the first time since 1290.

Abroad, commercial rivalry had led to a successful war with the Dutch from 1652-54.

Throughout the 1650s, treaties promoting foreign trade were signed with Sweden, Denmark, Portugal and France.

By the time of his death, Cromwell had strengthened Britain's diplomatic and military position within Europe.

He had also begun the process of creating a British worldwide trading empire and network of valuable colonies.

# CROMWELL

Oliver Cromwell (1599-1658) was the son of a Huntingdon landowner. He first entered parliament in 1628. When war broke out, he organised the cavalry in East Anglia. He became second-in-command of the New Model Army in 1645. After the execution of the king, Cromwell chaired the new Council of State until his death in 1658. Intensely religious, he believed he was carrying out God's will. Cromwell was also energetic, charming, and, contrary to popular belief, enjoyed hunting, music and other pastimes.

## FACT FILE

**THE PROTECTORATE 1653-1658**

**April 1653** Cromwell ends Rump Parliament; new Council of State set up, led by Cromwell

**July 1653** "Barebones" Parliament meets

**December 1653** Parliament dissolved; Instrument of Government becomes the new constitution of Protectorate; Cromwell made Lord Protector

**September 1654** First Protectorate Parliament

**April 1654** Dutch War ends

**January 1655** Cromwell dismisses parliament

**March 1655** Royalist rising in Wiltshire easily crushed

**August 1655** Cromwell divides country into 11 districts, each ruled by a major-general

**September 1656** Second Protectorate Parliament abolishes rule of major-generals

**May 1657** Cromwell accepts the Humble Petition and Advice as the new constitution but refuses the throne

**February 1658** Cromwell dismisses Second Protectorate Parliament

**September 1658** Oliver Cromwell dies

# The Restoration

Within two years of Oliver Cromwell's death, the republic ended and a Stuart king returned to rule the country. How did this extraordinary turn of events happen?

> **"That the government was and ought to be by Kings, Lords and Commons."**
>
> **Parliamentary resolution, 5 May 1660**

### THE END OF THE PROTECTORATE

When Cromwell died, Britain was strong economically and militarily. However, the government was weak, having depended entirely on Cromwell's power and authority. Many people felt that while he had been a good guardian of the country, he had also acted as a dictator, albeit a reluctant one. Royalists hated him as a regicide, while many republicans hated him because he had betrayed his radical beliefs and governed without parliament.

A few months before his death, Cromwell had named his son Richard as his successor. Richard was an able politician, but he lacked support. In January 1659 he recalled parliament to raise money to pay for the army. When the MPs criticized the army's role in government, the army chiefs forced Richard to dismiss parliament. Richard resigned shortly afterwards.

The army now found itself in charge of the country once again, but again found it difficult to form a government with which it could work.

In May 1659 they recalled the Rump Parliament — of whom only 78 members of the original 200 or so were still alive. However, these members argued with the army, which dismissed them and replaced parliament with a Committee of Safety composed of 23 civilian and military men chosen by the army.

There was a massive upsurge of protest at this action. Anti-army riots broke out in London and merchants refused to pay taxes until parliament was recalled. As law and order broke down across the country, General Monck, commander of the army in Scotland, demanded the recall of the Rump Parliament.

King Charles II. His restoration was a turning point in Britain's history and marked the end of the republic.

The navy and many soldiers supported Monck, so the army leaders were forced to recall the Rump yet again. Monck marched to London to support the Rump, but once there decided it lacked authority.

He therefore reversed Pride's Purge of December 1648, readmitting the expelled MPs to what now became the reinstated Long Parliament, on the condition that they voted to dissolve parliament and hold new elections.

## THE RETURN OF THE MONARCHY

By early 1660, Monck and his supporters were convinced that only the restoration of the monarchy would solve the crisis of government in Britain. They therefore opened negotiations with Charles II in exile in the Netherlands. Charles issued a declaration from his court at Breda promising a general pardon and limited religious freedom. He agreed to rely on the advice of parliament.

The newly elected Convention Parliament — so called because it convened itself — accepted the declaration and on 5 May 1660 agreed to restore Charles to the throne.

Through a combination of Charles's and Monck's astuteness, the political bankruptcy of both the army and the Rump Parliament, and near-anarchy in the country, the monarchy was restored and Britain's experiment with a republic came to an end.

# FACT FILE

## THE RESTORATION

September 1658 Richard Cromwell takes over as Lord Protector

January 1659 Parliament meets

April 1659 Army forces Richard to dismiss parliament

May 1659 Richard Cromwell resigns

May 1659 Army recalls Rump Parliament

October 1659 Army dissolves the Rump and sets up Committee of Safety to run country

December 1659 Monck demands the recall of parliament

December 1659 Rump parliament meets again

February 1660 Monck arrives in London from Scotland; expelled members of the Rump reinstated

March 1660 Long Parliament dissolved

April 1660 Charles II issues Declaration of Breda

April/May 1660 Convention Parliament opens; votes for restoration

25 May 1660 Charles lands at Dover; enters London 29 May

23 April 1661 Charles II crowned at Westminster Abbey

# CHARLES II

Charles II (1630-85), the eldest son of Charles I, fought for his father in the civil war before going into exile after 1645 in Jersey, France and the Netherlands. He returned to Scotland to reclaim his throne in 1650 but after his defeat at Worcester in 1651 he returned to the Netherlands. From there, he negotiated his restoration with General Monck before landing in Dover in May 1660.

He was crowned king in April 1661. Charles kept his throne while his father and his brother and successor (James II) lost theirs because he was a good judge of men. Although he was lazy and preferred pleasure to work, he remained popular with the people and had the political skill to avoid upsetting parliament.

# Causes and effects

**Although the main events of the civil wars are complex, historians do at least agree on what happened and when. What they are still arguing about, more than 300 years later, is what caused them.**

## WHY DID THEY HAPPEN?

1. The civil wars have traditionally been described as a conflict between king and parliament. The king believed in his divine right to rule, while parliament wished to increase the important role in government it had acquired in previous years. This makes it a conflict between an absolutist (dictatorial) king and a representative parliament.

2. Another way of looking at the conflict is to see it as a fight between a king who tried to centralise power in his hands in London and those in Scotland, Ireland and England who wished to govern themselves. First Scotland and then Ireland rebelled in defence of their religious liberties, as did England later to protect its parliamentary liberties. Thus the civil wars can be seen as a fight for religious and political liberty, as a conflict between central control and local freedoms, or between one king and his three very different kingdoms.

3. The wars can also be seen as a religious conflict. England and Wales had an episcopalian church, Scotland a presbyterian church, while Ireland was largely Catholic. Charles was a strict episcopalian, although many suspected him of being Catholic and resented his attempts to remodel both the English and Scottish churches in line with his own views.

In England, puritans who disliked the established church were also divided between presbyterians and Independents, the former dominating parliament, the latter the army. There were also other, smaller, religious sects and by the 1640s the British people were prepared to fight for the group they followed.

4. Many historians see the conflict not as constitutional or religious clash but as a class battle. The landed aristocracy wished to preserve their rights and privileges against a growing middle class of merchants, gentry and professional men who held power in parliament.

## CHRONOLOGY

### KEY EVENTS IN OUTLINE

**1639** First Bishops' War – Covenanter Scots v Charles I
**1640** Second Bishops' War
**1641-1650** Roman Catholic rebellion in Ireland v English protestant rulers and their Covenanter allies
**1642-1646** First English Civil War – parliament and the Covenanter Scots v Charles I and his Irish Catholic and Scottish royalist allies
**1648** Second English Civil War – parliament v Charles I and the Scots; royalist rebellions in England and Wales put down by parliament
**1649** Execution of Charles I; republic declared
**1649-1653** The Commonwealth
**1650-1651** Third English Civil War – parliament v Charles II and the Scots
**1653-1659** The Protectorate
**1660** Restoration of Charles II

The men of the middle classes also wished to have more say in government. Long-term economic and social changes in Britain brought these two classes into conflict. When war broke out, working people who were excluded from power altogether, such as soldiers and Levellers, also made their own views known. Some historians, however, disagree with this view and see the wars largely as a conflict within the governing class over who should run the country.

## WHAT ARE THEY CALLED?

The conflict used to be called the English Civil War, but that term is not favoured any more because it places England at the centre of the British Isles and ignores quite separate events in Scotland and Ireland. The terms Puritan or English Revolution are also misleading, because they only describe what went on in England after 1642.

Recently, historians have renamed the conflicts the Wars of the Three Kingdoms. This name reflects the fact that the wars began in Scotland and Ireland, not in England.

This view suggests that the civil wars within each kingdom were quite distinct from a three-kingdom, four-nation civil war that involved the entire British Isles.

The sense of national guilt at the execution of King Charles I was so great that after his death many people venerated him as a saint – the Royal Martyr.

## FACT FILE

KING v PARLIAMENT

**THE KING**
**Strengths**
• Commanded loyalty
• Drew support from the rich landed classes
• Strong in Wales and the west and north of England

**Weaknesses**
• Acted indecisively
• Failed to co-ordinate different supporters and their armies
• Lacked good military commanders
• Would not compromise his views to gain support
• Dependence on Catholic Irish lost him much support

**PARLIAMENT**
**Strengths**
• Held London, centre of national government
• Controlled southern England and the ports
• Set up New Model Army
• Able commanders in Fairfax and Cromwell
• Controlled many local militias and the navy
• Fervent support from presbyterians and Independents
• Scottish allies were crucial in First English Civil War

**Weaknesses**
• Divided between presbyterians and Independents
• Over-reliant on the army, which developed its own views
• Unable to gain mass consent for its policies
• Lacked legitimacy after execution of the king

# Glossary

| | |
|---|---|
| **Cavalier** | Royalist supporter of the king. |
| **Cessation, The** | Truce between the Confederation and government forces in Ireland, agreed in September 1643. |
| **Church of England** | The episcopal church of England and Wales, also known as the Anglican church. |
| **Confederation of Kilkenny** | The alliance of Catholic rebels in Ireland, set up in June 1642. |
| **Covenanter** | A Scottish presbyterian who supported the National Covenant against Charles I. |
| **Divine Right of Kings** | The belief that the king was divinely appointed and was answerable only to God for his actions. |
| **Episcopal** | System of church government in which the king appoints bishops, who in turn appoint the ministers (priests). |
| **Grandees** | Leaders of the New Model Army, such as Cromwell and Fairfax. |
| **Impeachment** | Trial by parliament of a government minister, often for treason or another major offence against the state. |
| **Independents** | Political and religious radicals who believed in the complete independence of the church from state control. |
| **Kirk** | The Scottish presbyterian church. |
| **Long Parliament** | The parliament first elected in November 1640 which sat until it was dismissed by Cromwell in April 1653; after Pride's Purge of presbyterian MPs in December 1648 it was known as the Rump Parliament. The Rump was recalled in May 1659 and was joined by its surviving expelled members to reform the Long Parliament in February 1660. It finally dissolved itself in March 1660. |
| **Monarchy** | Form of government with a hereditary king or queen as head of state. |

| | |
|---|---|
| **Parliament** | In both England and Ireland, parliament consisted of two houses: the House of Commons, where elected MPs sat, and the unelected House of Lords; in Scotland, parliament consisted of a single house containing both elected and unelected members. |
| **Presbyterian** | System of church government in which the ministers (priests) and bishops are elected by church members. |
| **Protestant** | A person who does not accept the supremacy of the Roman Catholic Church and worships at a presbyterian or episcopal church. |
| **Puritan** | A person who rejected episcopal government and believed in a purer, simpler form of worship. |
| **Regicide** | The killing or killer of a king. |
| **Republic** | Form of government when the people elect their head of state; opposite of monarchy. |
| **Roman Catholic Church** | The main Christian church in Western Europe, led by the pope in Rome. |
| **Roundhead** | A supporter of parliament and the army against the king. |
| **Royalist** | A supporter of the king against parliament. |
| **Rump Parliament** | see Long Parliament |
| **sect** | A small religious group. |
| **Stuarts** | The Scottish royal dynasty, or family, that inherited the English crown in 1603. |
| **suffrage** | The right to vote. |

## PICTURE CREDITS

AKG London: 11t.
Mary Evans Picture Library: 19t.
John C. Miles OLJ: 9t, 26b, 29b.
Peter Newark's Historical Pictures: 6-7t, 15t, 23t.
Deryc R Sands/Palace of Westminster Staff News: 12t.
Whilst every attempt has been made to clear copyright should there be any inadvertent omission please apply to the publisher regarding rectification.